HAL•LEONARD
INSTRUMENTAL
PLAY-ALONG

AUDIO
ACCESS
INCLUDED

PLAYBACK+
Speed • Pitch • Balance • Loop

FLUTE

CLASSIC POP SONGS

Audio arrangements by Peter Deneff

To access audio visit:
www.halleonard.com/mylibrary

Enter Code
6612-6242-4705-2082

ISBN 978-1-5400-0243-3

7777 W. BLUEMOUND RD. P.O. BOX 13819 MILWAUKEE, WI 53213

Visit Hal Leonard Online at
www.halleonard.com

BRIDGE OVER TROUBLED WATER

Flute

Words and Music by
PAUL SIMON

CANDLE IN THE WIND

Flute

Words and Music by ELTON JOHN
and BERNIE TAUPIN

Moderate Ballad

DUST IN THE WIND

Flute

Words and Music by
KERRY LIVGREN

EVERY BREATH YOU TAKE

FLUTE

Music and Lyrics by
STING

FIRE AND RAIN

Flute

Words and Music by
JAMES TAYLOR

HAVE I TOLD YOU LATELY

FLUTE

Words and Music by
VAN MORRISON

GOOD VIBRATIONS

FLUTE

Words and Music by BRIAN WILSON
and MIKE LOVE

HEAVEN

FLUTE

Words and Music by BRYAN ADAMS
and JIM VALLANCE

LEAN ON ME

Words and Music by
BILL WITHERS

Flute

SHE'S ALWAYS A WOMAN

FLUTE

Words and Music by
BILLY JOEL

Quickly, in 1

WITH A LITTLE HELP FROM MY FRIENDS

FLUTE

Words and Music by JOHN LENNON
and PAUL McCARTNEY

TEARS IN HEAVEN

Flute

Words and Music by ERIC CLAPTON
and WILL JENNINGS